Playing with Plays™
Presents
Shakespeare's

Julius Caesar
FOR KIDS
(The melodramatic version!)

For 5-17+ actors, or kids of all ages who want to have fun!
Creatively modified by
Brendan P. Kelso
Cover illustrations by Shana Hallmeyer,
and Ron Leishman

3 Melodramatic Modifications of Shakespeare's play
for 3 different group sizes:

5-10+ actors

8-13+ actors

11-20+ actors

Table Of Contents

To Shana;
For helping make my dream come true.
And the best darn illustrator EVER!

-Brendan

For performance rights please see page 6 of this book or contact:

contact@PlayingWithPlays.com

Foreword

When I was in high school there was something about Shakespeare that appealed to me. Not that I understood it mind you, but there were clear scenes and images that always stood out in my mind. Romeo & Juliet, "Romeo, Romeo; wherefore art thou Romeo?"; Julius Caesar, "Et tu Brute"; Macbeth, "Double, Double, toil and trouble"; Hamlet, "to be or not to be"; A Midsummer Night's Dream, all I remember about this was a wickedly cool fairy and something about a guy turning into a donkey that I thought was pretty funny. It was not until I started analyzing Shakespeare's plays as an actor that I realized one very important thing, I still didn't understand them. Seriously though, it's tough enough for adults, let alone kids. Then it hit me, why don't I make a version that kids could perform, but make it easy for them to understand with a splash of Shakespeare lingo mixed in? And voila! A melodramatic masterpiece was created! They are intended to be melodramatically fun!

THE PLAYS: There are 3 plays within this book, for three different group sizes. The reason: to allow educators or parents to get the story across to their children regardless of the size of their group. As you read through the plays, there are several lines that are highlighted. These are actual lines from the original book. I am a little more particular about the kids saying these lines verbatim. But the rest, well... have fun!

The entire purpose of this book is to instill the love of a classic story, as well as drama, into the kids.

And when you have children who have a passion for something, they will start to teach themselves, with or without school.

These plays are intended for pure fun. Please DO NOT have the kids learn these lines verbatim, that would be a complete waste of creativity. But do have them basically know their lines and improvise wherever they want as long as it pertains to telling the story. Because that is the goal of an actor: to tell the story. In A Midsummer Night's Dream, I once had a student playing Quince question me about one of her lines, "but in the actual story, didn't the Mechanicals state that 'they would hang us'?" I thought for a second and realized that she had read the story with her mom, and she was right. So I let her add the line she wanted and it added that much more fun, it made the play theirs. I have had kids throw water on the audience, run around the audience, sit in the audience, lose their pumpkin pants (size 30 around a size 15 doesn't work very well, but makes for some great humor!) and most importantly, die all over the stage. The kids love it.

One last note: if you want some educational resources, loved our plays, want to tell the world how much your kids loved performing Shakespeare, want to insult someone with our Shakespeare Insult Generator, or are just a fan of Shakespeare, then hop on our website and have fun:

PlayingWithPlays.com

With these notes, I'll see you on the stage, have fun, and break a leg!

SCHOOL, AFTERSCHOOL, and SUMMER classes

I've been teaching these plays as afterschool and summer programs for quite some time. Many people have asked what the program is, therefore, I have put together a basic formula so any teacher or parent can follow and have melodramatic success! As well, many teachers use my books in a variety of ways. You can view the formula and many more resources on my website at: PlayingWithPlays.com

ROYALTIES

I am asked all the time about royalties for my plays. So, here are the basic rules:

1) Please contact me! I always LOVE to hear about a school or group performing my books!

2) If you are a group and DO NOT charge your kids to be in this production: contact me, and we can talk about waiving the book costs or discounts on signed copies.

3) If you are a group and DO NOT charge the audience to see the plays, there is no royalty! (but, please leave a positive review, and send some photos!)

4) If you are a group and DO charge your kids to be in the production, contact me as I will give you a bulk discount (8 books or more), sign each book, and send some really cool press on Shakespeare tattoos!

5) If you are a group and DO charge the audience to see the performance, please contact me to discuss royalty options.

Any other questions or comments, please email me at:

contact@PlayingWithPlays.com

The 15-Minute or so Julius Caesar

By William Shakespeare
creatively edited by Brendan P. Kelso
5-10+ Actors

CAST OF CHARACTERS:

[1]**JULIUS CAESAR:** The tyrant dude

MARK ANTONY: Ruler after Caesar

[2]**OCTAVIUS:** Ruler after Caesar

BRUTUS: Caesar's ex-friend

CASSIUS: another ex-friend

[2]**PINDARUS:** Cassius' slave

[2]**LUCIUS:** Brutus' slave

[2]**SOOTHSAYER:** a fortune-teller

[1]**CAESAR'S GHOST:** he's a dead Caesar

[3]**TOWNSFOLK:** townsfolk

The same actors can play the following parts:

[1]CAESAR and GHOST
[2]OCTAVIUS can also play SOOTHSAYER, PINDARUS, and LUCIUS
[3]TOWNSFOLK can be as many extras as needed
[3]Play can also be run with NO Townsfolk

ACT 1 SCENE 1

(CAESAR, BRUTUS, CASSIUS, and ANTONY enter)

CASSIUS: *(to audience)* Peace, ho! Caesar speaks.

CAESAR: Ahh, what a great day Antony. I just fought Pompey and won! People are dancing in the streets over my victory, and I am now the ruler of Rome!

ANTONY: Yes, Caesar, you are the man. When Caesar says 'do this,' it is perform'd. Now don't let this go to your head!

CAESAR: Yeah, yeah, yeah. *(enter SOOTHSAYER)*

SOOTHSAYER: *(in a really spooky creepy voice)* Caesar!

CAESAR: What? Who said my name?

SOOTHSAYER: Beware the Ides of March!

BRUTUS: It is a soothsayer. And I think he is telling you to beware the Ides of March.

CAESAR: What the heck is the Ides of March?

ANTONY: It's March 15th.

CAESAR: Whatever.

SOOTHSAYER: *(to the point)* Listen, it means watch your back, or you might find a knife in it!

CAESAR: Huh, that's nice.

SOOTHSAYER: *(in a spooky creepy voice again)* Beware the Ides of March!

CAESAR: He is a dreamer, let us leave him. *(ALL exit but BRUTUS and CASSIUS)*

CASSIUS: Brutus, I know Caesar is your friend, but he acts as if he were a god.

(offstage cries of 'hip-hip hooray' for Caesar)

CASSIUS: I fear the future of Rome with Caesar in charge.

BRUTUS: Listen Cassius, Caesar is my friend. What are you worried about?

CASSIUS: You are of the same rank as Caesar, why him, and not you?

BRUTUS: *(confused)* I need to think about that one.

(CAESAR and ANTONY enter and are downstage away from BRUTUS and CASSIUS)

ANTONY: Caesar, Cassius was acting rather strange earlier.

CAESAR: Yeah, he thinks too much, such men are dangerous, and he creeps me out. I don't trust him.

ANTONY: Let's get out of here. *(CAESAR and ANTONY exit)*

BRUTUS: Cassius, the crowd tried to crown Caesar three times today, but he refused.

CASSIUS: I am telling you, he is trouble!

BRUTUS: No, the people of Rome like Caesar more because he will not take the crown.

CASSIUS: Yeah, well I still think he is trouble.

BRUTUS: Why don't you come over later and we will talk about it. *(BRUTUS exits)*

CASSIUS: *(to audience)* I need to take down Caesar! Hmmm, must think of an evil plan to deceive Brutus and turn him against Caesar. MUAH-HA-HA-HA!!!!

(CASSIUS exits laughing evilly)

(CASSIUS enters)

CASSIUS: *(to audience)* I have recruited a team to conspire against Caesar, but I still need to have Brutus on my side. I need to leave these cleverly crafted evil letters around for him to find. Once he reads them, he will join me! *(CASSIUS exits laughing evilly again)*

ACT 2 SCENE 1

(BRUTUS and LUCIUS enter)

BRUTUS: Lucius, my servant, I have not slept since Caesar got back in town. I am afraid Caesar might use his new found power in a bad way. If he does, that would be a terrible thing!

LUCIUS: That would be very bad. Oh look, *(pointing offstage)* mail's here! *(LUCIUS runs offstage and returns with letter and hands letter to BRUTUS)* Hey Brutus, someone delivered this random letter.

BRUTUS: *(reads letter)* "Caesar is bad" That's it! I will resolve to kill Caesar to save Rome from what he might do.

LUCIUS: Hey, just a reminder, tomorrow is March 15th.

BRUTUS: Well wouldn't you know it, the Ides of March! Now I am going to do a very bad thing, I must hide it in smiles. *(enter CASSIUS)*

BRUTUS: I'm in! *(they high five each other and do a cheer 'conspirators!')*

CASSIUS: Hey, I think we need to kill Antony, too.

BRUTUS: Antony, nah, he's a wimp.

ANTONY: *(offstage)* Hey!

BRUTUS: Don't worry about him.

CASSIUS: I am worried that Caesar will be superstitious and not come out tomorrow.

BRUTUS: Why don't you send him one of those letters you like to write?

CASSIUS: Great idea! Now let's laugh evilly as we exit!

(ALL exit, laughing evilly)

(CAESAR enters)

CAESAR: My wife is freaking me out. Three times last night she screamed in her sleep, 'Help ho, they murder Caesar'. My wife will not let me out of the house today! Ohhh, that woman has an iron fist! *(to audience)* I am not afraid of death. Now my wife, that's something else. Okay, I'll stay.

(a crumpled piece of paper is thrown on stage to Caesar)

CAESAR: Hmmm, what's this. Oh, it's a letter. *(starts reading and talking to himself)* "You need to go to the capitol today", *(to himself)* ummm, I don't think I am going to go today, *(keeps reading)* "you have to go! Everybody is waiting for you." *(looks at letter a little stunned, then starts talking to letter)* Yeah, well my wife had this bad dream and kept saying, 'Help ho, they murder Caesar', and it really gave me the creeps, and that soothsayer yesterday, too. *(continues reading letter)* "But the Senate is going to crown you today."

CAESAR: Crown? Did you say, "crown"? Hmmm....well then, I'm going! Who cares what my wife tried to warn me about!

(CAESAR exits)

ACT 3 SCENE 1

(CAESAR, BRUTUS, CASSIUS, and SOOTHSAYER enter)

CAESAR: *(to Soothsayer)* The Ides of March are come. *(mocking Soothsayer and dancing around)* And look at me, I'm still here! Neener, neener, neener!!!

SOOTHSAYER: Ay, Caesar, but not gone. In other words, continue watching your back, buddy!

CAESAR: Whatever, I will be crowned today!

SOOTHSAYER: You should listen to my warning.

(BRUTUS and CASSIUS are slowly circling CAESAR)

CAESAR: Why are you guys staring at me with those funny looks on your faces? And those sharp swords pointed at.......me.

SOOTHSAYER: I'm outta here! Tried to warn you!

(SOOTHSAYER exits; BRUTUS and CASSIUS start stabbing CAESAR)

CAESAR: *(to audience after some stabbing)* This really hurts. *(to Brutus)* Et tu, Brute?! *(all stop)*

BRUTUS: Huh? What does that mean?

CAESAR: It's Latin for 'You too Brutus?' Sheesh!

BRUTUS: Oh.....yeah *(BRUTUS delivers final blow)*

CASSIUS: Well we did it, we have freed Rome!

(ANTONY enters and kneels next to Caesar)

ANTONY: O mighty Caesar! Dost thou lie so low? What did you guys do here? What a mess!

BRUTUS: Caesar was my friend, but I did this for Rome!

ANTONY: You do realize that you just started a civil war?

CASSIUS: Hmmm, we didn't think about that.

(ALL exit, CAESAR left on stage)

ACT 3 SCENE 2

(ANTONY, BRUTUS, and CASSIUS enter. TOWNSFOLK enter audience area)

CASSIUS: I don't trust letting Antony speak at Caesar's funeral.

BRUTUS: Don't worry, I have it under control. *(addresses audience)* Dear Romans, I know it looks bad that we murdered Caesar, but it is not that I loved Caesar less, but that I loved Rome more. That is why he needed to kick the bucket. Now please, listen to your new leader, Antony.

ANTONY: *(addresses audience)* Friends, Romans, countrymen, lend me your ears; I come to bury Caesar, not to praise him. But truth be told, Brutus is wrong! Caesar wasn't a bad guy.

(TOWNSFOLK say things like, "O noble Caesar", "O woeful day", "O most bloody site", "we will be revenged".)

ANTONY: Now listen, this is how good Caesar was, in his will, he left all of you money! *(ANTONY throws money into the audience)* So, I think revenge is in order!

(TOWNSFOLK say things like, "we will burn the house of BRUTUS", "Away then, come, seek the conspirators" TOWNSFOLK exit.)

BRUTUS: I am leaving Rome!

CASSIUS: Me too!

(ALL exit)

(enter BRUTUS and CASSIUS very mad at each other; LUCIUS follows)

CASSIUS: Brutus, most noble brother, you have done me wrong and that makes me very mad at you.

BRUTUS: What did I do? How should I wrong a brother? You were the one who tricked me into killing Caesar with that letter! You are very greedy and corrupt, the same reason we killed Caesar! The name of Cassius honours this corruption.

CASSIUS: *(very mad)* Don't talk to me that way, it hurts my feelings.

BRUTUS: You have a very bad temper... and bad breath.

CASSIUS: You're right, I do have a bad temper, I feel bad about it, would you kill me? *(tries to hand his sword to BRUTUS)*

BRUTUS: No, now we have work to do. *(a girl's scream is heard from offstage)*

CASSIUS: What was that?

BRUTUS: I think that was my wife's scream, let me check. *(BRUTUS peeks offstage)* That was my wife and she just killed herself from guilt and stress. Portia is dead.

CASSIUS: Bummer. Sorry, good buddy.

BRUTUS: That's okay.

CASSIUS: Good night, my lord. *(CASSIUS exits)*

BRUTUS: Hey Lucius, play me some music.

LUCIUS: Nah, I'm tired. *(goes to sleep)*

(CAESAR'S GHOST enters)

BRUTUS: Aghhhhh! Speak to me, who are you?

CAESAR'S GHOST: Thou evil spirit, Brutus. I am the ghost of Caesar. You are a very bad man.

BRUTUS: Go away.

CAESAR'S GHOST: Okay.

(ALL exit)

ACT 5 SCENE 1

(BRUTUS and CASSIUS enter from one side of the stage and OCTAVIUS and ANTONY from the other side)

ANTONY: Octavius, look over there, it is Brutus and Cassius. Let's go get them!

OCTAVIUS: Okay. Which one of you killed Caesar?

(BRUTUS and CASSIUS point at each other)

ANTONY: They both did.

OCTAVIUS: I am here to avenge Caesar's death, if you dare fight today. So which one of you want to die first?

(BRUTUS and CASSIUS point at each other)

CASSIUS: You know this is my birthday, so you should kill him first.

BRUTUS: Man, you are ruthless.

CASSIUS: Hey, every man for himself. *(CASSIUS and BRUTUS run offstage for their lives)*

ANTONY: Don't you hate chickens?

(ALL exit chasing)

(CASSIUS and PINDARUS enter)

CASSIUS: Pindarus, my slave, this just doesn't look good. My soldiers have deserted me and I am left alone.

PINDARUS: Nope, really doesn't. You need to fly further off, my lord, fly further off!

CASSIUS: This hill is far enough. O, coward that I am, I need to check out. Would you kill me?

PINDARUS: Sure, but do I get to go free after you're gone?

CASSIUS: Yes! Now be a free man. *(hands sword to Pindarus)*

PINDARUS: Great! So I am free! *(takes sword and kills him. Then runs offstage not sure of what he just did)*

(BRUTUS enters)

BRUTUS: Ahhhh man. He is slain. *(to audience)* A moment of silence, please. *(no time passes)* Okay, now back to the battle.

(BRUTUS exits)

ACT 5 SCENE 3

(BRUTUS enters)

BRUTUS: My army is getting knocked around pretty bad by Antony's army. I can't stand being here anymore, I need to die, *(stabs himself)* farewell. Caesar, now be still; I killed not thee with half so good of will. *(BRUTUS dies)*

(enter OCTAVIUS and ANTONY)

OCTAVIUS: Well, looks as if our work is done here. I feel bad for Brutus.

ANTONY: Yeah, Brutus was the only man who was doing what he thought was best for Rome. All the conspirators, save only he, did what they did in envy of great Caesar. Let's go home!

(ALL exit)

THE END

The 20-Minute or so Julius Caesar

By William Shakespeare
creatively edited by Brendan P. Kelso
8-13+ Actors

CAST OF CHARACTERS:

[1]**JULIUS CAESAR:** The tyrant dude

MARK ANTONY: Ruler after Caesar

[2]**OCTAVIUS:** Ruler after Caesar

BRUTUS: Caesar's ex-friend

CASSIUS: another ex-friend

DECIUS: another ex-friend

[3]**PINDARUS:** Cassius' slave

[3]**LUCIUS:** Brutus' slave

[2,3]**POMPEY:** the first loser to Caesar

NARRATOR: A narrator

[1]**CAESAR'S GHOST:** he's a dead Caesar

[2,3]**SOOTHSAYER:** a fortune-teller

[4]**TOWNSFOLK:** townsfolk

The same actors can play the following parts:

[1]CAESAR and GHOST

[2]OCTAVIUS, POMPEY, and SOOTHSAYER

[3]SOOTHSAYER, PINDARUS, POMPEY, and LUCIUS

[4]TOWNSFOLK can be as many extras as needed

[4]Play can also be run with NO Townsfolk

ACT 1 SCENE 1

NARRATOR: Once upon a time in ancient Rome there was a great battle. *(CAESAR and POMPEY enter fighting.)* In this corner, Caesar, and in this corner, Pompey.

POMPEY: Attack!

(NARRATOR does play by play of fight, POMPEY is killed)

NARRATOR: And Caesar wins! *(CAESAR exits triumphantly)*

NARRATOR: People are dancing in the streets over Caesar's win.

(TOWNSFOLK cross stage dancing and hollering, saying great things about Caesar. TOWNSFOLK drag POMPEY offstage)

(CAESAR, BRUTUS, CASSIUS, and ANTONY enter)

CASSIUS: *(to audience)* Peace, ho! Caesar speaks.

CAESAR: Ahh, what a great day Antony, I am now the ruler of Rome!

ANTONY: Yes, Caesar, you are the man. Now don't let this go to your head!

CAESAR: Yeah, yeah, yeah. *(enter SOOTHSAYER)*

SOOTHSAYER: *(in a really spooky creepy voice)* Caesar!

CAESAR: What? Who said my name?

SOOTHSAYER: Beware the Ides of March!

BRUTUS: It is a soothsayer. And I think he is telling you to beware the Ides of March.

CAESAR: What the heck is the Ides of March?

ANTONY: It's March 15th.

CAESAR: Whatever.

SOOTHSAYER: *(to the point)* Listen, it means watch your back, or you might find a knife in it!

CAESAR: Huh, that's nice.

SOOTHSAYER: *(in a spooky creepy voice again)* Beware the Ides of March!

CAESAR: He is a dreamer, let us leave him. *(ALL exit but BRUTUS and CASSIUS)*

CASSIUS: Brutus, I know Caesar is your friend, but he acts as if he were a god.

(offstage cries of 'hip-hip hooray' for Caesar)

CASSIUS: I fear the future of Rome with Caesar in charge.

BRUTUS: Listen Cassius, Caesar is my friend. What are you worried about?

CASSIUS: You are of the same rank as Caesar, why him, and not you?

BRUTUS: *(confused)* I need to think about that one.

(CAESAR and ANTONY enter and are downstage away from BRUTUS and CASSIUS)

ANTONY: Caesar, Cassius was acting rather strange earlier.

CAESAR: Yeah, he thinks too much, such men are dangerous, and he creeps me out. I don't trust him.

ANTONY: Let's get out of here. *(CAESAR and ANTONY exit)*

BRUTUS: Cassius, the crowd tried to crown Caesar three times today, but he refused.

CASSIUS: I am telling you, he is trouble!

BRUTUS: No, the people of Rome like Caesar more because he will not take the crown.

CASSIUS: Yeah, well I still think he is trouble.

BRUTUS: Why don't you come over later and we will talk about it. *(BRUTUS exits)*

CASSIUS: *(to audience)* I need to take down Caesar! Hmmm, must think of an evil plan to deceive Brutus and turn him against Caesar. MUAH-HA-HA-HA!!!!

(CASSIUS exits laughing evilly)

ACT 1 SCENE 2

NARRATOR: *(referencing Cassius)* He doesn't seem
very nice. The word on the streets is that Cassius has
recruited other people to conspire against Caesar.
Cassius is working on his plot to turn Brutus against
Caesar. *(enter CASSIUS)*

CASSIUS: *(to audience)* I need to leave these cleverly
crafted evil letters around for Brutus to find. Once he
reads them, he will join me!

(CASSIUS exits laughing evilly again)

NARRATOR: *(enter BRUTUS)* Brutus is hanging out in his orchard. It is three in the morning. Three in the morning? Why are you not asleep, better yet, why am I not asleep? Anyway, he hasn't slept since Caesar got back in town. *(enter LUCIUS)*

BRUTUS: Lucius, my servant, I am afraid Caesar might use his new found power in a bad way. If he does, that would be a terrible thing!

LUCIUS: That would be very bad. Oh look, *(pointing offstage)* mail's here! *(LUCIUS runs offstage and returns with letter and hands letter to BRUTUS)* Hey Brutus, someone delivered this random letter.

BRUTUS: *(reads letter)* "Caesar is bad" That's it! I will resolve to kill Caesar to save Rome from what he might do.

LUCIUS: Hey, just a reminder, tomorrow is March 15th.

BRUTUS: Well wouldn't you know it, the Ides of March! Now I am going to do a very bad thing, I must hide it in smiles. *(enter CASSIUS, and DECIUS)*

BRUTUS: I'm in! *(they high five each other and do a cheer 'conspirators!')*

NARRATOR: *(to audience)* What you see before you is the group of conspirators against Caesar.

LUCIUS: *(to audience)* Not me! I'm outta here!

(LUCIUS exits)

CASSIUS: Great, this is Decius, he is a conspirator against Caesar too.

DECIUS: Hello.

CASSIUS: Hey, I think we need to kill Antony, too.

BRUTUS: Antony, nah, he's a wimp.

ANTONY: *(offstage)* Hey!

BRUTUS: Don't worry about him.

CASSIUS: I am worried that Caesar will be superstitious and not come out tomorrow.

DECIUS: Don't worry, I will go over to Caesar's house, and bring him to the capitol tomorrow morning. I will deceive him.

CASSIUS: Great! Then let's laugh evilly as we exit!

(ALL exit, laughing evilly)

NARRATOR: The next morning, at Caesar's house. *(CAESAR enters)*

CAESAR: My wife is freaking me out. Three times last night she screamed in her sleep, 'Help ho, they murder Caesar'. My wife will not let me out of the house today!

NARRATOR: The wife has an iron fist!

CAESAR: I am not afraid of death. *(to audience)* Now my wife, that's something else. Okay, I'll stay. *(enter DECIUS)*

CAESAR: Hello, Decius.

DECIUS: Caesar, I have come to take you to the capitol today.

CAESAR: Ohh, um...I'm not going today.

DECIUS: What? But everybody is waiting for you.

CAESAR: Yeah, well my wife had this bad dream and kept saying, 'Help ho, they murder Caesar', and it really gave me the creeps, and that soothsayer yesterday, too.

DECIUS: Is that what your wife said? No, no, no. It means if you DON'T come and help, they will murder you. You have to come, the Senate is going to crown you today.

CAESAR: Crown? Did you say, "crown"?

DECIUS: Yeah, a nice shiny crown.

CAESAR: Well, why didn't you say so in the first place! Let's go!

(DECIUS and CAESAR exit)

NARRATOR: Your wife tried to warn you!

ACT 3 SCENE 1

NARRATOR: Later that day. The capitol.

(CAESAR, BRUTUS, CASSIUS, DECIUS, and SOOTHSAYER enter)

CAESAR: *(to Soothsayer)* The Ides of March are come. *(mocking Soothsayer and dancing around)* And look at me, I'm still here! Neener, neener, neener!!!

SOOTHSAYER: Ay, Caesar, but not gone. In other words, continue watching your back, buddy!

CAESAR: Whatever, I will be crowned today!

SOOTHSAYER: You should listen to my warning.

(Conspirators are slowly circling Caesar)

NARRATOR: *(to Caesar)* Would you listen to the soothsayer?

CAESAR: Be quiet narrator, you are not even part of the story.

NARRATOR: Sorry.

CAESAR: *(suddenly noticing everyone around him)* Why are you guys all around me with those funny looks on your faces? And all of those sharp swords pointed at.......me.

SOOTHSAYER: I'm outta here! Tried to warn you!

(SOOTHSAYER exits; ALL start stabbing CAESAR)

CAESAR: *(to audience after some stabbing)* This really hurts. *(to Brutus)* Et tu, Brute?! *(all stop)*

BRUTUS: Huh? What does that mean?

CAESAR: It's Latin for 'You too Brutus?' Sheesh!

BRUTUS: Oh.....yeah *(BRUTUS delivers final blow)*

NARRATOR: *(to Caesar)* I told you to listen to her! *(CAESAR flashes sword at NARRATOR as he finally dies; TOWNSFOLK run across stage screaming in pandemonium)* There is pandemonium on the streets!

CASSIUS: Well we did it, we have freed Rome!

(ANTONY enters and kneels next to Caesar)

ANTONY: O mighty Caesar! Dost thou lie so low? What did you guys do here? What a mess!

BRUTUS: Caesar was my friend, but I did this for Rome!

NARRATOR: Nice friend.

(BRUTUS glares and shows sword at narrator who quickly hides behind podium)

ANTONY: You do realize that you just started a civil war?

CASSIUS: Hmmm, we didn't think about that.

(ALL exit, CAESAR left on stage)

NARRATOR: *(to audience)* Later that day, Caesar's funeral, and you are all Romans at the funeral. This is where we have interactive theater, so please join along to make it more fun!

(ANTONY, BRUTUS, CASSIUS, and DECIUS enter. TOWNSFOLK enter audience area)

CASSIUS: I don't trust letting Antony speak at Caesar's funeral.

BRUTUS: Don't worry, I have it under control. *(addresses audience)* Dear Romans, I know it looks bad that we murdered Caesar, but it is not that I loved Caesar less, but that I loved Rome more. That is why he needed to kick the bucket.

(NARRATOR shows 'boo' card to audience)

BRUTUS: Now please, listen to your new leader, Antony.

ANTONY: *(addresses audience)* Friends, Romans, countrymen, lend me your ears; I come to bury Caesar, not to praise him. But truth be told, Brutus is wrong! Caesar wasn't a bad guy.

(TOWNSFOLK say things like, "O noble Caesar", "O woeful day", "O most bloody site", "we will be revenged".)

ANTONY: Now listen, this is how good Caesar was, in his will, he left all of you money!

(ANTONY throws money into the audience; NARRATOR shows 'applause' card to audience)

ANTONY: So, I think revenge is in order!

(NARRATOR starts the 'revenge' chant, BRUTUS and CASSIUS flash swords at NARRATOR, but after seeing the hostile audience, BRUTUS and CASSIUS flee the scene. TOWNSFOLK say things like, "we will burn the house of BRUTUS", "Away then, come, seek the conspirators" TOWNSFOLK exit.)

BRUTUS: I am leaving Rome!

CASSIUS and DECIUS: Me too!

(ALL exit, NARRATOR drags CAESAR'S body offstage)

NARRATOR: Well, it is really getting tense on the streets now. People are screaming for justice *(people scream)* to what the conspirators did to Caesar. Meanwhile, Antony meets with Octavius, another new ruler of Rome, and are preparing for war against Brutus and Cassius. Speaking of Brutally Brutus and Careless Cassius they are currently at their wits end in Brutus' tent.

(enter BRUTUS and CASSIUS very mad at each other; LUCIUS follows)

CASSIUS: Brutus, most noble brother, you have done me wrong and that makes me very mad at you.

BRUTUS: What did I do? How should I wrong a brother? You were the one who tricked me into killing Caesar with that letter! You are very greedy and corrupt, the same reason we killed Caesar! The name of Cassius honours this corruption.

CASSIUS: *(very mad)* Don't talk to me that way, it hurts my feelings.

BRUTUS: You have a very bad temper... and bad breath.

NARRATOR: Hello. *(getting their attention)* Hi, yes, I have a friend that is a shrink. Maybe he can help. His phone number is...... *(starts talking until he sees CASSIUS and BRUTUS glaring and pointing swords at him)*

CASSIUS: What is it with this guy?

BRUTUS: I don't know, maybe we should kill him? *(they hold swords at throat of NARRATOR)*

NARRATOR: Whoa.....Hey listen, I know where I am not wanted. Let me just go back to storytelling. Right over there. *(NARRATOR quickly makes his way back to the podium)*

CASSIUS: Now, where were we? Oh yes, you're right, I do have a bad temper, I feel bad about it, would you kill me? *(tries to hand his sword to BRUTUS)*

BRUTUS: No, now we have work to do. *(a girl's scream is heard from offstage)*

CASSIUS: What was that?

BRUTUS: I think that was my wife's scream, let me check. *(BRUTUS peeks offstage)* That was my wife and she just killed herself from guilt and stress. Portia is dead.

CASSIUS: Bummer. Sorry, good buddy.

BRUTUS: That's okay.

NARRATOR: Now that they are buddy-buddy, they start plotting how to take on Octavius and Antony. Cassius leaves Brutus to go to sleep.

CASSIUS: Good night, my lord. *(CASSIUS exits)*

BRUTUS: Hey Lucius, play me some music.

LUCIUS: Nah, I'm tired. *(goes to sleep)*

(CAESAR'S GHOST enters)

BRUTUS: Aghhhhh! Speak to me, who are you?

CAESAR'S GHOST: Thou evil spirit, Brutus. I am the ghost of Caesar. You are a very bad man.

BRUTUS: Go away.

CAESAR'S GHOST: Okay.

(ALL exit)

(BRUTUS and CASSIUS enter from one side of the stage and OCTAVIUS and ANTONY from the other side)

NARRATOR: The battlefield. Octavius and Antony happen to run into Brutus and Cassius in the immense combat zone.

OCTAVIUS: Okay, which one of you killed Caesar?

(BRUTUS and CASSIUS point at each other)

ANTONY: They both did.

OCTAVIUS: I am here to avenge Caesar's death, if you dare fight today. So which one of you want to die first?

(BRUTUS and CASSIUS point at each other)

CASSIUS: You know this is my birthday, so you should kill him first.

BRUTUS: Man, you are ruthless.

CASSIUS: Hey, every man for himself. *(CASSIUS and BRUTUS run offstage for their lives)*

ANTONY: Don't you hate chickens?

(ALL exit chasing)

NARRATOR: Well, this is just getting ugly. Let's see, according to our man on the field, there are some battles taking place just outside of Rome. It looks as if Octavius' army is getting weak, but we just got confirmation that Cassius' soldiers have fled the scene in the middle of the battle.

(enter CASSIUS and PINDARUS)

CASSIUS: Pindarus, my slave, this just doesn't look good.

PINDARUS: Nope, really doesn't. You need to fly further off, my lord, fly further off!

CASSIUS: This hill is far enough. O, coward that I am, I need to check out. Would you kill me?

PINDARUS: Sure, but do I get to go free after you're gone?

CASSIUS: Yes! Now be a free man. *(hands sword to Pindarus)*

PINDARUS: Great! So I am free! *(takes sword and kills him. Then runs offstage not sure of what he just did)*

NARRATOR: Ouch, that looks like it hurt. *(BRUTUS enters)*

BRUTUS: Ahhhh man. He is slain. *(to audience)* A moment of silence, please. *(no time passes)* Okay, now back to the battle.

(BRUTUS exits)

ACT 5 SCENE 3

NARRATOR: Okay, well I just got word that Brutus' army is getting knocked around pretty bad by Antony's army. So bad that Brutus wants to take his own life, but can't find anyone to do it.

(enter BRUTUS)

BRUTUS: *(to narrator)* Hey, do you mind killing me?

NARRATOR: No, I am the narrator; I am not part of the story.

BRUTUS: Yeah, you sure didn't act like it during the play.

NARRATOR: Don't start getting brave with me.

BRUTUS: You know, I have nothing to lose, and you are buggn' me *(kills NARRATOR and then holds up 'applause' sign to audience)*

BRUTUS: Now, where was I? Oh yes, *(stabs himself)* farewell. Caesar, now be still; I killed not thee with half so good of will. *(BRUTUS dies)*

(enter OCTAVIUS and ANTONY)

OCTAVIUS: Well, looks as if our work is done here. I feel bad for Brutus.

ANTONY: Yeah, Brutus was the only man who was doing what he thought was best for Rome. All the conspirators, save only he, did what they did in envy of great Caesar. Let's go home!

(ALL exit)

THE END

The 25-Minute or so Julius Caesar

By William Shakespeare

creatively edited by Brendan P. Kelso

11-20+ Actors

CAST OF CHARACTERS:

[1]**JULIUS CAESAR** – The tyrant dude

[2]**CALPURNIA** – Caesar's Wife

MARK ANTONY – Ruler after Caesar

[5]**OCTAVIUS** – Ruler after Caesar

BRUTUS – Caesar's ex-friend

CASSIUS – another ex-friend

CINNA – another ex-friend

[3]**DECIUS** – another ex-friend

[5]**CASCA** – another ex-friend

[2]**PORTIA** – Brutus' wife

[4]**PINDARUS** - Cassius' slave

[4]**LUCIUS** – Brutus' slave

[3]**POMPEY** – the first loser to Caesar

NARRATOR – A narrator

[4]**SOOTHSAYER** – a fortune-teller

[3]**CINNA THE POET** – A poet

[1]**CAESAR'S GHOST**: he's a dead Caesar

[6]**TOWNSFOLK** – townsfolk

[7]**HENCHMEN** - Pompey's henchmen - they die

The same actors can play the following parts:

[1]CAESAR and GHOST

[2]CALPURNIA and PORTIA

[3]POMPEY, CINNA THE POET, and DECIUS

[4]SOOTHSAYER, PINDARUS, and LUCIUS

[5]CASCA and OCTAVIUS

[6]TOWNSFOLK can be as many extras as needed

[7]Pompey can also have HENCHMEN if needed

ACT 1 SCENE 1

NARRATOR: Once upon a time in ancient Rome there was a great battle. *(CAESAR, POMPEY, and 2 HENCHMEN enter fighting)* In this corner, Caesar, and in this corner, Pompey.

POMPEY: Attack!

(NARRATOR does play by play of fight; HENCHMEN attack first and are killed; then POMPEY attacks and is killed)

NARRATOR: And Caesar wins! *(CAESAR exits triumphantly)*

NARRATOR: People are dancing in the streets over Caesar's win.

(TOWNSFOLK cross stage dancing and hollering, saying great things about Caesar)

(CAESAR, CALPURNIA, BRUTUS, CASCA, CASSIUS, and ANTONY enter)

CASCA: *(to audience)* Peace, ho! Caesar speaks.

CAESAR: Ahh, what a great day Antony, I am now the ruler of Rome!

ANTONY: Yes, Caesar, you are the man.

CALPURNIA: Caesar dear, now don't let this go to your head, okay.

CAESAR: Yes, dear. *(enter SOOTHSAYER)*

SOOTHSAYER: *(in a really spooky creepy voice)* Caesar!

CAESAR: What? Who said my name?

SOOTHSAYER: Beware the Ides of March!

BRUTUS: It is a soothsayer. And I think he is telling you to beware the Ides of March.

CAESAR: What the heck is the Ides of March?

CALPURNIA: It's March 15th, dear.

CAESAR: Whatever.

SOOTHSAYER: *(to the point)* Listen, it means watch your back, or you might find a knife in it!

CAESAR: Huh, that's nice.

SOOTHSAYER: *(in a spooky creepy voice again)* Beware the Ides of March!

CAESAR: He is a dreamer, let us leave him. *(ALL exit but BRUTUS and CASSIUS)*

CASSIUS: Brutus, I know Caesar is your friend, but he acts as if he were a god.

(offstage cries of 'hip-hip hooray' for Caesar)

CASSIUS: I fear the future of Rome with Caesar in charge.

BRUTUS: Listen Cassius, Caesar is my friend. What are you worried about?

CASSIUS: You are of the same rank as Caesar, why him, and not you?

BRUTUS: *(confused)* I need to think about that one.

(CAESAR and ANTONY enter and are downstage away from BRUTUS and CASSIUS)

ANTONY: Caesar, Cassius was acting rather strange earlier.

CAESAR: Yeah, he thinks too much, such men are dangerous, and he creeps me out. I don't trust him.

ANTONY: Let's get out of here. *(CAESAR and ANTONY exit; CASCA enters)*

BRUTUS: Casca, my friend, what is all the cheering about?

CASCA: Well Brutus, the crowd tried to crown Caesar three times today, but he refused.

CASSIUS: I am telling you, he is trouble!

CASCA: No, the people of Rome like Caesar more because he will not take the crown!

CASSIUS: Yeah, well I still think he is trouble.

BRUTUS: Why don't you come over later and we will talk about it. *(BRUTUS exits)*

CASSIUS: *(to audience)* I need to take down Caesar! Hmmm, must think of an evil plan to deceive Brutus and turn him against Caesar. *(looks at CASCA)* Hey Casca, we need to take down Caesar!

CASCA: *(shrugs shoulders)* Okay.

(ALL exit laughing evilly)

ACT 1 SCENE 2

NARRATOR: *(referencing Casca and Cassius)* They don't seem very nice. The word on the streets is that Cassius has recruited other people to conspire against Caesar. Cassius is working with Cinna, another conspirator, on his plot to turn Brutus against Caesar. *(enter CASSIUS and CINNA)*

CASSIUS: Cinna, listen my friend; I need you to deliver this cleverly crafted evil letter to Brutus. Once he reads it, he will join us!

CINNA: Okay boss.

(ALL exit)

NARRATOR: *(enter BRUTUS)* Brutus is hanging out in his orchard. It is three in the morning. Three in the morning? Why are you not asleep, better yet, why am I not asleep? Anyway, he hasn't slept since Caesar got back in town. *(enter LUCIUS)*

BRUTUS: Lucius, my servant, I am afraid Caesar might use his new found power in a bad way. If he does, that would be a terrible thing!

LUCIUS: That would be very bad. *(enter CINNA)*

CINNA: *(hands letter to BRUTUS)* Hey Brutus, here is a letter from Cassius.

BRUTUS: *(reads letter)* "Caesar is bad" That's it! I will resolve to kill Caesar to save Rome from what he might do.

LUCIUS: Hey, just a reminder, tomorrow is March 15th.

BRUTUS: Well wouldn't you know it, the Ides of March! Now I am going to do a very bad thing, I must hide it in smiles. *(enter CASSIUS, CASCA, and DECIUS)*

CASCA: So?

BRUTUS: I'm in! *(they high five each other and do a cheer 'conspirators!')*

NARRATOR: *(to audience)* What you see before you is the group of conspirators against Caesar.

LUCIUS: *(to audience)* Not me! I'm outta here!

(LUCIUS exits)

CASSIUS: Great, this is Decius, he is a conspirator against Caesar too.

DECIUS: Hello.

CASCA: Hey, I think we need to kill Antony, too.

BRUTUS: Antony, nah, he's a wimp.

ANTONY: *(offstage)* Hey!

BRUTUS: Don't worry about him.

CASSIUS: I am worried that Caesar will be superstitious and not come out tomorrow.

DECIUS: Don't worry, I will go over to Caesar's house, and bring him to the capitol tomorrow morning. I will deceive him.

CASSIUS: Great! Then let's laugh evilly as we exit! *(ALL exit, laughing evilly, except BRUTUS; PORTIA and LUCIUS enter)*

NARRATOR: The wife!

PORTIA: Brutus my lord. You have been a real pain since yesterday, what's up?

BRUTUS: Portia! What mean you? Wherefore rise you now? Ahhh...I'm not feeling good? *(LUCIUS shaking head behind BRUTUS)*

PORTIA: Nice try, now tell me why you are up this late?

BRUTUS: Indigestion? *(LUCIUS shaking head behind BRUTUS)*

PORTIA: You used that one last night, why won't you tell me the truth, who were those visitors that were just here?

BRUTUS: Trick or treaters? *(LUCIUS tries again, but BRUTUS quickly looks back)*

PORTIA: It's March. Look, I love you, but you are buggn' me. Now go to bed!

BRUTUS: Yes, dear. *(BRUTUS exits)*

PORTIA: Lucius, I want you to follow Brutus tomorrow and tell me what he is up to.

LUCIUS: Okay.

(PORTIA and LUCIUS exit)

ACT 2 SCENE 2

NARRATOR: The next morning, at Caesar's house. *(CAESAR enters)*

CAESAR: My wife is freaking me out. Three times last night Calpurnia screamed in her sleep, 'Help ho, they murder Caesar'. *(CALPURNIA enters)*

CALPURNIA: Caesar, I have a bad feeling about today.

CAESAR: Yeah, I know, you woke me up. Okay, see ya!

CALPURNIA: You shall not stir out of your house today.

CAESAR: Cowards die many times before their deaths, the valiant never taste of death but once.

CALPURNIA: *(demanding)* You will stay here as I say!

NARRATOR: The wife has an iron fist!

CAESAR: I am not afraid of death. *(to audience)* Now my wife, that's something else. Okay, I'll stay. *(enter DECIUS)*

CAESAR: Hello, Decius.

DECIUS: Caesar, I have come to take you to the capitol today.

CAESAR: Ohh, um...I'm not going today.

DECIUS: What? But everybody is waiting for you.

CAESAR: Yeah well, my wife had this bad dream and kept saying, 'Help ho, they murder Caesar', and it really gave me the creeps, and that soothsayer yesterday, too.

DECIUS: Is that what your wife said? No, no, no. It means if you DON'T come and help, they will murder you. You have to come, the Senate is going to crown you today.

CAESAR: Crown? Did you say, "crown"?

DECIUS: Yeah, a nice shiny crown.

CAESAR: Well, why didn't you say so in the first place! Let's go! *(DECIUS and CAESAR exit)*

CALPURNIA: You should listen to me! Bye dear!

(CALPURNIA exits)

NARRATOR: She tried to warn you!

ACT 3 SCENE 1

NARRATOR: Later that day. The capitol.

(CAESAR, BRUTUS, LUCIUS, CASSIUS, DECIUS, CINNA, CASCA, and SOOTHSAYER enter)

CAESAR: *(to Soothsayer)* The Ides of March are come. *(mocking Soothsayer and dancing around)* And look at me, I'm still here! Neener, neener, neener!!!

SOOTHSAYER: Ay, Caesar, but not gone. In other words, continue watching your back, buddy!

CAESAR: Whatever, I will be crowned today!

SOOTHSAYER: You should listen to my warning.

(CONSPIRATORS are slowly circling Caesar)

NARRATOR: *(to Caesar)* Would you listen to the soothsayer?

CAESAR: Be quiet narrator, you are not even part of the story.

NARRATOR: Sorry.

CAESAR: Why are you guys all around me with those funny looks on your faces? And all of those sharp swords pointed at.......me.

SOOTHSAYER: I'm outta here! Tried to warn you!

(SOOTHSAYER exits; ALL start stabbing CAESAR)

CAESAR: *(to audience after some stabbing)* This really hurts. *(to Brutus)* Et tu, Brute?! *(all stop)*

BRUTUS: Huh? What does that mean?

CAESAR: It's Latin for 'You too Brutus?' Sheesh!

BRUTUS: Oh.....yeah *(BRUTUS delivers final blow)*

NARRATOR: *(to Caesar)* I told you to listen to her! *(CAESAR flashes sword at NARRATOR as he finally dies; TOWNSFOLK run across stage screaming in pandemonium)* There is pandemonium on the streets!

CASSIUS: Well we did it, we have freed Rome!

(ANTONY enters and kneels next to Caesar, LUCIUS exits)

ANTONY: O mighty Caesar! Dost thou lie so low? What did you guys do here? What a mess!

BRUTUS: Caesar was my friend, but I did this for Rome!

NARRATOR: Nice friend.

(BRUTUS glares and shows sword at narrator who quickly hides behind podium)

ANTONY: You do realize that you just started a civil war?

CASCA: Hmmm, *(asking CASSIUS)* Did we think about that?

(CASSIUS shakes head 'no' ALL exit, CAESAR left on stage)

ACT 3 SCENE 2

NARRATOR: *(to audience)* Later that day, Caesar's funeral, and you are all Romans at the funeral. This is where we have interactive theater, so please join along to make it more fun!

(ANTONY, BRUTUS, CASSIUS, CINNA, and DECIUS enter. TOWNSFOLK enter audience area)

CASSIUS: I don't trust letting Antony speak at Caesar's funeral.

BRUTUS: Don't worry, I have it under control. *(addresses audience)* Dear Romans, I know it looks bad that we murdered Caesar, but it is not that I loved Caesar less, but that I loved Rome more. That is why he needed to kick the bucket.

(NARRATOR shows 'boo' card to audience)

BRUTUS: Now please, listen to your new leader, Antony.

ANTONY: *(addresses audience)* Friends, Romans, countrymen, lend me your ears; I come to bury Caesar, not to praise him. But truth be told, Brutus is wrong! Caesar wasn't a bad guy.

(TOWNSFOLK say things like, "O noble Caesar", "O woeful day", "O most bloody site", "we will be revenged".)

ANTONY: Now listen, this is how good Caesar was, in his will, he left all of you money!

(ANTONY throws money into the audience; NARRATOR shows 'applause' card to audience)

ANTONY: So, I think revenge is in order!

(NARRATOR starts the 'revenge' chant, BRUTUS and CASSIUS flash swords at NARRATOR, but after seeing the hostile audience, BRUTUS and CASSIUS flee the scene. TOWNSFOLK say things like, "we will burn the house of BRUTUS", "Away then, come, seek the conspirators" TOWNSFOLK exit.)

BRUTUS: I am leaving Rome!

CASSIUS, DECIUS, CINNA: Me too!

(BRUTUS, CINNA, DECIUS, and CASSIUS exit)

NARRATOR: This is where trouble starts to happen. Enter the innocent bystander.

(CINNA THE POET enters, along with TOWNSFOLK)

TOWNSFOLK: Hey, what is your name? Aren't you Cinna the conspirator against Caesar?

CINNA THE POET: Nope, I am Cinna the Poet.

NARRATOR: He happens to have the same name as one of the conspirators, poor chap.

TOWNSFOLK: We think you are one of the conspirators against Caesar, tear him to pieces!!! *(they kill CINNA THE POET)*

CINNA THE POET: NOOOOOOOOOOOOOOO! Don't you know it, I am Cinna the poet! *(dying in extreme agony)*

(NARRATOR drags body offstage)

(LUCIUS and PORTIA enter)

PORTIA: Did you follow Brutus?

LUCIUS: Yep

PORTIA: So?

LUCIUS: Well, Brutus killed Caesar and then skipped town when the townsfolk started getting mad and saying something like: "We will burn the house of Brutus".

PORTIA: Wait, that's this house. Do you smell smoke?

LUCIUS: Yeah, I'm outta here! *(LUCIUS exits)*

PORTIA: This is bad, very bad, not good.

(PORTIA exits)

NARRATOR: Well, it is really getting tense on the streets now. People are screaming for justice *(people scream)* to what the conspirators did to Caesar. Meanwhile, Antony meets with Octavius, another new ruler of Rome, and are preparing for war against Brutus and Cassius. Speaking of Brutally Brutus and Careless Cassius they are currently at their wits end in Brutus' tent.

(enter BRUTUS and CASSIUS very mad at each other; LUCIUS follows)

CASSIUS: Brutus, most noble brother, you have done me wrong and that makes me very mad at you.

BRUTUS: What did I do? How should I wrong a brother? You were the one who tricked me into killing Caesar with that letter! You are very greedy and corrupt, the same reason we killed Caesar! The name of Cassius honours this corruption.

CASSIUS: *(very mad)* Don't talk to me that way, it hurts my feelings.

BRUTUS: You have a very bad temper... and bad breath.

NARRATOR: Hello. *(getting their attention)* Hi, yes, I have a friend that is a shrink. Maybe he can help. His phone number is...... *(starts talking until he sees CASSIUS and BRUTUS glaring and pointing swords at him)*

CASSIUS: What is it with this guy?

BRUTUS: I don't know, maybe we should kill him? *(they hold swords at throat of NARRATOR)*

NARRATOR: Whoa.....Hey listen, I know where I am not wanted. Let me just go back to storytelling. Right over there. *(NARRATOR quickly makes his way back to the podium)*

CASSIUS: Now, where were we? Oh yes, you're right, I do have a bad temper, I feel bad about it, would you kill me? *(tries to hand his sword to BRUTUS)*

BRUTUS: No, now we have work to do. *(PORTIA screams offstage)*

CASSIUS: What was that?

BRUTUS: I think that was my wife's scream.

(PORTIA runs on stage and dies with sword in her)

BRUTUS: Huh, that was my wife and she just killed herself from guilt and stress. Portia is dead.

CASSIUS: Bummer. Sorry, good buddy.

BRUTUS: That's okay. Hey Narrator, make yourself useful and clean this up.

NARRATOR: My job is to tell stories and that's it! *(CASSIUS and BRUTUS quickly glare at him)* Okay, okay. *(drags body offstage)* I didn't sign up for this!

NARRATOR: Now that they are buddy-buddy, they start plotting how to take on Octavius and Antony. Cassius leaves Brutus to go to sleep.

CASSIUS: Good night, my lord. *(CASSIUS exits)*

BRUTUS: Hey Lucius, play me some music.

LUCIUS: Nah, I'm tired. *(goes to sleep)*

(CAESAR'S GHOST enters)

BRUTUS: Aghhhhh! Speak to me, who are you?

CAESAR'S GHOST: Thou evil spirit, Brutus. I am the ghost of Caesar. You are a very bad man.

BRUTUS: Go away.

CAESAR'S GHOST: Okay.

(ALL exit)

(BRUTUS and CASSIUS enter from one side of the stage and OCTAVIUS and ANTONY from the other side)

NARRATOR: The battlefield. Octavius and Antony happen to run into Brutus and Cassius in the immense combat zone.

OCTAVIUS: Okay, which one of you killed Caesar?

(BRUTUS and CASSIUS point at each other)

ANTONY: They both did.

OCTAVIUS: I am here to avenge Caesar's death, if you dare fight today. So which one of you want to die first?

(BRUTUS and CASSIUS point at each other)

CASSIUS: You know this is my birthday, so you should kill him first.

BRUTUS: Man, you are ruthless.

CASSIUS: Hey, every man for himself. *(CASSIUS and BRUTUS run offstage for their lives)*

ANTONY: Don't you hate chickens?

(ALL exit chasing)

NARRATOR: Well, this is just getting ugly. Let's see, according to our man on the field, there are some battles taking place just outside of Rome. It looks as if Octavius' army is getting weak, but we just got confirmation that Cassius' soldiers have fled the scene in the middle of the battle.

(enter CASSIUS and PINDARUS)

CASSIUS: Pindarus, my slave, this just doesn't look good.

PINDARUS: Nope, really doesn't. You need to fly further off, my lord, fly further off!

CASSIUS: This hill is far enough. O, coward that I am, I need to check out. Would you kill me?

PINDARUS: Sure, but do I get to go free after you're gone?

CASSIUS: Yes! Now be a free man. *(hands sword to Pindarus)*

PINDARUS: Great! So I am free! *(takes sword and kills him. Then runs offstage not sure of what he just did)*

NARRATOR: Ouch, that looks like it hurt. *(BRUTUS enters)*

BRUTUS: Ahhhh man. He is slain. *(to audience)* A moment of silence, please. *(no time passes)* Okay, now back to the battle.

(BRUTUS exits)

NARRATOR: Okay, well I just got word that Brutus' army is getting knocked around pretty bad by Antony's army. So bad that Brutus wants to take his own life, but can't find anyone to do it.

(enter BRUTUS)

BRUTUS: *(to narrator)* Hey, do you mind killing me?

NARRATOR: No, I am the narrator; I am not part of the story.

BRUTUS: Yeah, you sure didn't act like it during the play.

NARRATOR: Don't start getting brave with me.

BRUTUS: You know, I have nothing to lose, and you are buggn' me *(kills NARRATOR and then holds up 'applause' sign to audience)*

BRUTUS: Now, where was I? Oh yes, *(stabs himself)* farewell. Caesar, now be still; I killed not thee with half so good of will. *(BRUTUS dies)*

(enter OCTAVIUS and ANTONY)

OCTAVIUS: Well, looks as if our work is done here. I feel bad for Brutus.

ANTONY: Yeah, Brutus was the only man who was doing what he thought was best for Rome. All the conspirators, save only he, did what they did in envy of great Caesar. Let's go home!

(ALL exit)

THE END

SPECIAL THANKS

This thanks is to all the kids who have melodramtically performed *Julius Caesar for Kids* over the years. I have watched and learned from each of you and have woven in your creative, and humorus additions!

Thank you for making this all worthwhile!

Sneak Peeks at other Playing With Plays books:

The Jungle Book for Kids

PARENT WOLF: Oh hi, Bagheera. What's happening in the life of a panther?

BAGHEERA: I wanted to warn you. Shere Khan's in town again.

PARENT WOLF: The tiger? What's he doing in this part of the jungle?

BAGHEERA: What tigers do. You know, hunt, eat, hunt again, eat... hunt...eat... *(trailing off)*

PARENT WOLF: *(play-acting like a tiger)* Oh look at me, I'm a mean ol' tiger, roar!!! *(there is a LOUD ROAR and GROWL from offstage, PARENT WOLF is a bit shocked)*

BAGHEERA: Listen! That's him now!

(enter MOWGLI, running off-balance, and falling down)

PARENT WOLF: Whoa! A man's cub! Look! *(all turn to look at MOWGLI)* How little and so... smelly, but cute! *(starts petting his hair)*

(BAGHEERA sneaks over to MOWGLI and whispers something in his ear. MOWGLI sighs and gets down on his knees to appear smaller; he remains on his knees throughout the rest of the scene and ACT1 SCENE 2)

MOWGLI: *(very sarcastically)* Gaa gaa. Goo goo.

(SHERE KHAN enters. PARENT WOLF hides MOWGLI behind her back)

SHERE KHAN: A man's cub went this way. Its parents have run off. Give it to me. I'll uh... take care of him... *(as he rubs his belly)* you can TOTALLY trust me! *(gives* *the audience a big evil smile)*

PARENT WOLF: You are NOT the boss of us.

SHERE KHAN: Excuse me?! Do you know who I am? It is I, Shere Khan, who speaks! I'm kind of a big deal. And scary! GRRRRR.

PARENT WOLF: The man's cub is mine; he shall not be killed! So beat it; you don't scare us.

SHERE KHAN: Fine. But I'll get him some day, make no mistake! Muahahahahaha! ROAR! *(SHERE KHAN exits)*

PARENT WOLF: *(to MOWGLI)* Mowgli the Frog I will call thee. Lie still, little frog.

MOWGLI: *(to PARENT WOLF)* Frog?

PARENT WOLF: *(to MOWGLI and audience)* Yeah, I guess Rudyard Kipling liked frogs! But now we have to see what the wolf leader says.

(enter AKELA, BAGHEERA, and BALOO)

AKELA: Okay, wolves, let's get this meeting started! Howl!

WOLVES: Howl!! *(all WOLVES howl)*

PARENT WOLF: Akela, our great leader, I'd like to present the newest member of our pack, Mowgli the Frog!

AKELA: Hmmm, Frog, huh? If you say so.

(enter SHERE KHAN)

SHERE KHAN: ROAR! The cub is mine! Give him to me!

AKELA: Who speaks for this cub?

BALOO: *(speaking in a big, deep bear voice!)* I, Baloo the Bear, I speak for the man's cub. I myself will teach him the ways of the jungle.

Hamlet for Kids

(enter GERTRUDE and POLONIUS)

GERTRUDE: What's up, Polonius?

POLONIUS: I am going to hide and spy on your conversation with Hamlet!

GERTRUDE: Oh, okay.

(POLONIUS hides somewhere, enter HAMLET very mad, swinging his sword around)

HAMLET: MOM!!! I AM VERY MAD!

GERTRUDE: Ahhh! You scared me!

(POLONIUS sneezes from hiding spot)

HAMLET: *(not seeing POLONIUS)* How now, a rat? Who's hiding? *(stabs POLONIUS)*

POLONIUS: O, I am slain! Ohhhh the pain! *(dies on stage)*

GERTRUDE: Oh me, what has thou done?

HAMLET: Oops, I thought that was Claudius. Hmph, oh well... as I was saying, I AM MAD you married uncle Claudius!

GERTRUDE: Oh that, yeah, sorry. *(in a motherly voice)* Now, you just killed Polonius, clean up this mess and go to your room!

HAMLET: Okay Mom.

(all exit, HAMLET drags POLONIUS' body offstage)

ACT 4 SCENES 1-3

(enter GERTRUDE and CLAUDIUS)

GERTRUDE: Ahhh, Dear?

CLAUDIUS: Yeah?

GERTRUDE: Ummmm, you would not believe what I have seen tonight! Polonius is dead.

CLAUDIUS: WHAT!?

GERTRUDE: Yeah, Hamlet was acting a little crazy, Polonius sneezed or something, then Hamlet yelled, "A rat, a rat!" and then WHACK! It was over.

CLAUDIUS: *(very angry)* HAMLET!!!! GET OVER HERE NOW!!!!!

(enter HAMLET)

CLAUDIUS: *(very casual)* Hey, what's up?

HAMLET: What noise, who calls on Hamlet? What do you want?

CLAUDIUS: Now, Hamlet. Where's Polonius' body?

HAMLET: I'm not telling!

CLAUDIUS: Oh come on, please tell me!!! Please! With a cherry on top! Where is Polonius?

HAMLET: Oh, all right. He's over there, up the stairs into the lobby. *(points offstage)*

(POLONIUS enters and dies again)

CLAUDIUS: Ewe... he's a mess! Hamlet, I am sending you off to England.

HAMLET: Fine! Farewell, dear Mother. And I'm taking this with me! *(HAMLET grabs POLONIUS and drags him offstage)*

(all exit but CLAUDIUS)

CLAUDIUS: *(to audience)* I have arranged his execution in England! *(laughs evilly as he exits)* Muwahahaha...

Henry V for Kids

ACT 2 SCENE 2

(enter BEDFORD and EXETER, observing CAMBRIDGE and SCROOP, who whisper among themselves)

BEDFORD: Hey Exeter, do you think it's a good idea that King Henry is letting those conspirators wander around freely?

EXETER: It's alright, Bedford. King Henry has a plan! He knows EVERYTHING they are plotting. BUT, they don't KNOW he knows. And HE knows that they don't know he knows...and...

BEDFORD: *(interrupting)* Okay, okay, I get it. Let's go sit in the audience and watch! *(they sit in the audience; enter HENRY)*

HENRY: Greetings, my good and FAITHFUL friends, Cambridge and Scroop. Perfect timing! I need your advice on something.

CAMBRIDGE: Sure thing. You know we'd do anything for you! Never was a monarch better feared and loved.

SCROOP: That's why we're going to kick some French butt!! *(SCROOP and CAMBRIDGE high-five)*

HENRY: Excellent! A man was arrested yesterday for shouting nasty things about me. But I'm sure by now he's thought better of it. I think I ought to show mercy and pardon him.

SCROOP: Nah, let him be punished.

HENRY: Ahhh, but let us yet be merciful.

CAMBRIDGE: Nah, I'm with Scroop! Off with his head!

HENRY: Is that your final answer?

CAMBRIDGE & SCROOP: YES!

HENRY: Ok, but if we don't show mercy for small offenses, how will we show mercy for big ones? I will release him. Now, take a look at THESE LETTERS.

(as CAMBRIDGE and SCROOP read the letters, their jaws drop)

HENRY: Why, how now, gentlemen? What see you in those papers that your jaws hang so low?

EXETER: *(to audience)* The letters betray their guilt!

CAMBRIDGE: I do confess my fault...

SCROOP:....and do submit me to your Highness' mercy! *(they start begging and pleading on the ground)*

HENRY: Exeter, Bedford, arrest these traitors. What did they say... Oh yeah, OFF WITH THEIR HEADS!

CAMBRIDGE: Whoa there!

SCROOP: Off with our what? What happened to the whole "mercy" thing you were just talking about!?

HENRY: Your own words talked me out of it! Take them away!

CAMBRIDGE: Well, this stinks!

(EXETER and BEDFORD arrest CAMBRIDGE and SCROOP; ALL exit, except HENRY)

HENRY: Being king is no fun sometimes. Scroop used to be one of my best friends. *(SCROOP runs on stage and dies melodramatically)* But there's no time to mope! *(CAMBRIDGE runs on stage and dies on top of SCROOP)* The signs of war advance. No king of England, if not King of France! NOW CLEAN UP THIS MESS!

(EXETER and BEDFORD run on stage and drag bodies off; exit HENRY)

Two Gentlemen of Verona for Kids

ANTONIO: It's not nothing.

PROTEUS: Ahhhhh......It's a letter from Valentine, telling me what a great time he's having in Milan, yeah... that's what it says!

ANTONIO: Awesome! Glad to hear it! Because, you leave tomorrow to join Valentine in Milan.

PROTEUS: What!? Dad! No way! I don't want... I mean, I need some time. I've got some things to do.

ANTONIO: Like what?

PROTEUS: You know...things! Important things! And stuff! Lots of stuff!

ANTONIO: No more excuses! Go pack your bag. *(ANTONIO begins to exit)*

PROTEUS: Fie!

ANTONIO: What was that?

PROTEUS: Fiiii......ne with me, Pops! *(ANTONIO exits)* I was afraid to show my father Julia's letter, lest he should take exceptions to my love; and my own lie of an excuse made it easier for him to send me away.

ANTONIO: *(Offstage)* Proteus! Get a move on!!

PROTEUS: Fie!!!

(exit)

ACT 2 SCENE 1

(enter VALENTINE and SPEED following)

VALENTINE: Ah, Silvia, Silvia! *(heavy sighs)*

SPEED: *(mocking)* Madam Silvia! Madam Silvia! Gag me.

VALENTINE: Knock it off! You don't know her.

SPEED: Do too. She's the one that you can't stop staring at. Makes me wanna barf.

VALENTINE: I do not stare!

SPEED: You do. AND you keep singing that silly love song. *(sing INSERT SAPPY LOVE SONG)* You used to be so much fun.

VALENTINE: Huh? *(heavy sigh, starts humming SAME LOVE SONG)*

SPEED: Never mind.

VALENTINE: I have loved her ever since I saw her. Here she comes!

SPEED: Great. *(to audience)* Watch him turn into a fool.

(enter SILVIA)

VALENTINE: Hey, Silvia.

SILVIA: Hey, Valentine. What's goin' on?

VALENTINE: Nothin'. What's goin' on with you?

SILVIA: Nothin'.

(pause)

VALENTINE: What are you doing later?

SILVIA: Not sure. Prob-ly nothin'. You?

VALENTINE: Me neither. Nothin'.

SILVIA: Yea?

VALENTINE: Probably.

SPEED: *(to audience)* Kill me now.

SILVIA: Well, I guess I better go.

VALENTINE: Oh, okay! See ya'..

(pause)

SILVIA: See ya' later maybe?

VALENTINE: Oh, yea! Maybe! Yea! Okay!

SILVIA: Bye.

VALENTINE: Bye!

(exit SILVIA)

SPEED: *(aside)* Wow. *(to VALENTINE)* Dude, what the heck was that?

VALENTINE: I think she has a boyfriend. I can tell.

SPEED: Dude! She is so into you! How could you not see that?

VALENTINE: Do you think?

SPEED: Come on. We'll talk it through over dinner. *(to audience)* Fool. Am I right?

(exit)

The Three Musketeers for Kids

(ATHOS and D'ARTAGNAN enter)

ATHOS: Glad you could make it. I have engaged two of my friends as seconds.

D'ARTAGNAN: Seconds?

ATHOS: Yeah, they make sure we fight fair. Oh, here they are now!

(enter ARAMIS and PORTHOS singing, "Bad boys, bad boys, watcha gonna do...")

PORTHOS: Hey! I'm fighting him in an hour. I am going to fight... because...well... I am going to fight!

ARAMIS: And I fight him at two o'clock! Ours is a theological quarrel. *(does a thinking pose)*

D'ARTAGNAN: Yeah, yeah, yeah... I'll get to you soon!

ATHOS: We are the Three Musketeers; Athos, Porthos, and Aramis.

D'ARTAGNAN: Whatever, Ethos, Pathos, and Logos, let's just finish this! *(swords crossed and are about to fight; enter JUSSAC and cardinal's guards)*

PORTHOS: The cardinal's guards! Sheathe your swords, gentlemen.

JUSSAC: Dueling is illegal! You are under arrest!

ARAMIS: *(to ATHOS and PORTHOS)* There are five of them and we are but three.

D'ARTAGNAN: *(steps forward to join them)* It appears to me we are four! I have the spirit; my heart is that of a Musketeer.

PORTHOS: Great! I love fighting!

(Musketeers say "Fight, fight fight!...Fight, fight, fight!" as they are fighting; D'ARTAGNAN fights JUSSAC and it's the big fight; JUSSAC is wounded and exits; the 3 MUSKETEERS cheer)

ATHOS: Well done! Let's go see Treville and the king!

ARAMIS: And we don't have to kill you now!

PORTHOS: And let's get some food, too! I'm hungry!

D'ARTAGNAN: *(to audience)* This is fun!

(ALL exit)

ACT 2 SCENE 1

(enter 3 MUSKETEERS, D'ARTAGNAN, and TREVILLE)

TREVILLE: The king wants to see you, and he's not too happy you killed a few of the cardinal's guards.

(enter KING)

KING: *(yelling)* YOU GUYS HUMILIATED THE CARDINAL'S GUARDS!

ATHOS: Sire, they attacked us!

KING: Oh...Well then, bravo! I hear D'Artagnan beat the cardinal's best swordsman! Brave young man! Here's some money for you. Enjoy! *(hands money to D'ARTAGNAN)*

D'ARTAGNAN: Sweet!

(ALL exit)

Richard III for Kids

ACT 1 SCENE 4

(CLARENCE is in prison, sleeping. He wakes up from a bad dream)

CLARENCE: Terrible, horrible, no good, very bad dream! *(pauses, notices audience and addresses them)* O, I have pass'd a miserable night! I dreamt that Richard was trying to kill me! Hahahaha, Richard is SUCH a good guy, he would NEVER do a thing like that!

(enter MURDERER carrying a weapon)

MURDERER: I sounded like such a pro, no one will know it's my first day on the job! Hehehe!

CLARENCE: Hey! Who's there?

MURDERER: Um... um... *(hides his murder weapon behind his back)*

CLARENCE: Your eyes do menace me. Are you planning to murder me? 'Cause that's not a good idea. My brother Richard is a REALLY powerful guy.

MURDERER: Ha! Richard is the one who sent me here to do this! *(a pause)* Whoops...

CLARENCE: Hahaha, you foolish fellow. Richard loves me.

MURDERER: Dude, what are you not getting? He PAID me to do this!

CLARENCE: O, do not slander him, for he is kind.

(The MURDERER stabs CLARENCE. CLARENCE dies a dramatic death)

CLARENCE: Kinda ruthless... *(dies)*

MURDERER: *(Gasps)* Oh, my! He's dead! I feel bad now... I bet Clarence was a really nice guy. Ahhh, the guilt! Wow, I should have stayed in clown school.

(MURDERER exits)

ACT 2 SCENE 1

(KING EDWARD is surrounded by QUEEN ELIZABETH and BUCKINGHAM)

KING EDWARD: Well, this has been a great day at work! Everyone's agreed to get along!

(ELIZABETH and BUCKINGHAM shake hands with each other to celebrate the peace. Enter RICHARD. KING EDWARD smiles happily)

KING EDWARD: If I die, I will be at peace! But I must say I'm feeling a lot healthier after all of this peace-making!

RICHARD: Hey! Looks like you're all in a good mood. That's great, 'cause you know I LOVE getting along! So what's up?

KING EDWARD: I made them like each other!

RICHARD: How lovely! I like you all now, too! Group hug? *(everyone shakes their head)* No? *(he grins sweetly)*

ELIZABETH: Wonderful! Once Clarence gets back from the Tower, everything will be perfect!

RICHARD: WHAT??? We make peace and then you insult us like this? That's no way to talk about a DEAD man!!

(EVERYONE gasps)

KING EDWARD: Is Clarence dead? I told them to cancel the execution!

RICHARD: Oh, yeah... guess that was too late! *(winks to audience)*

KING EDWARD: Nooooooo!!!! Oh my poor brother! Now I feel more sick than EVER! Oh, poor Clarence!

(All exit except RICHARD and BUCKINGHAM)

RICHARD: Well, that sure worked as planned!

BUCKINGHAM: Great job, partner!

(both exit, laughing evilly)

Sneak peek of
Christmas Carol
for Kids

(enter GHOST PRESENT wearing a robe and holding a turkey leg and a goblet)

GHOST PRESENT: Wake up, Scrooge! I am the Ghost of Christmas Present. Look upon me!

SCROOGE: I'm looking. Not that impressed. But let's get on with it.

GHOST PRESENT: Touch my robe! *(SCROOGE touches GHOST PRESENT's robe. Pause. They look at each other)* Er...it must be broken. Guess we walk. Come on. *(they begin walking downstage)*

SCROOGE: Where are we going?

GHOST PRESENT: Your employee, Bob Cratchit's house. Oh look, here we are.

(enter BOB, MRS. CRATCHIT, MARTHA CRATCHIT, and TINY TIM, who has a crutch in one hand; they are all holding bowls)

BOB: *(to audience)* Hi, we're the Cratchit family. We are a REALLY happy family!

MRS. CRATCHIT: *(to audience)* Yes, but we're REALLY poor, too. Thanks to HIS boss! *(pointing at BOB)*

MARTHA: *(to audience)* Yeah, as you can see our bowls are empty. *(shows empty bowl)* We practically survive off air.

TINY TIM: *(to audience)* But we're happy!

MRS. CRATCHIT: *(to audience; overly sappy)* Because we have each other.

TINY TIM: And love!

SCROOGE: *(to GHOST PRESENT)* Seriously, are they for real?

GHOST PRESENT: Yep! Adorable, isn't it?

BOB: A merry Christmas to us all.

TINY TIM: God bless us every one!

SCROOGE: Spirit, tell me if Tiny Tim will live.

GHOST PRESENT: *(puts hands to head as if looking into the future)* Ooooo, not so good...I see a vacant seat in the poor chimney corner, and a crutch without an owner. If SOMEBODY doesn't change SOMETHING, the child will die.

SCROOGE: No, no! Say he will be spared.

GHOST PRESENT: Nope, can't do that, sorry. Unless SOMEONE decides to change... hint, hint.

BOB: A Christmas toast to my boss, Mr. Scrooge! The founder of the feast!

MRS. CRATCHIT: *(angrily)* Oh sure, Mr. Scrooge! If he were here I'd give him a piece of my mind to feast upon. What an odious, stingy, hard, unfeeling man!

BOB: Dear, it's Christmas day. He's not THAT bad. *(Pause)* He's just... THAT sad. *(BOB holds up his bowl)* Come on, kids, to Scrooge! He probably needs it more than us!

MARTHA & TINY TIM: *(holding up their bowls)* To Scrooge!

MRS. CRATCHIT: *(muttering)* Thanks for nothing.

BOB: That's not nice.

MARTHA: And we Cratchits are ALWAYS nice. Read the book, Mom.

MRS. CRATCHIT: Sorry.

(the CRATCHIT FAMILY exits)

SCROOGE: She called me odious! Do I really smell that bad?

GHOST PRESENT: Odious doesn't mean you stink. Although in this case you do... According to the dictionary, odious means "unequivocally detestable." I mean, you are a toad sometimes Mr. Scrooge.

SCROOGE: Wow... that's kind of... mean.

Treasure Island for Kids

(enter JIM, TRELAWNEY, and DOCTOR; enter CAPTAIN SMOLLETT from the other side of the stage)

TRELAWNEY: Hello Captain. Are we all shipshape and seaworthy?

CAPTAIN: Trelawney, I don't know what you're thinking, but I don't like this cruise; and I don't like the men.

TRELAWNEY: *(very angry)* Perhaps you don't like the ship?

CAPTAIN: Nope, I said it short and sweet.

DOCTOR: What? Why?

CAPTAIN: Because I heard we are going on a treasure hunt and the coordinates of the island are: *(whispers to DOCTOR)*

DOCTOR: Wow! That's exactly right!

CAPTAIN: There's been too much blabbing already.

DOCTOR: Right! But, I doubt ANYTHING will go wrong!

CAPTAIN: Fine. Let's sail!

(ALL exit)

Act 2 Scene 3

(enter JIM, SILVER, and various other pirates)

SILVER: Ay, ay, mates. You know the song: Fifteen men on the dead man's chest.

ALL PIRATES: Yo-ho-ho and a bottle of rum!

(PIRATES slowly exit)

JIM: *(to the audience)* So, the Hispaniola had begun her voyage to the Isle of Treasure. As for Long John, well, he still is the nicest cook...

SILVER: Do you want a sandwich?

JIM: That would be great, thanks Long John! *(SILVER exits; JIM addresses audience)* As you can see, Long John is a swell guy! Until...

(JIM hides in the corner)

Act 2 Scene 4

(enter SILVER and OTHER PIRATES)

JIM: *(to audience)* I overheard Long John talking to the rest of the pirates.

SILVER: Listen here you, Scallywags! I was with Captain Flint when he hid this treasure. And those cowards have the map. Follow my directions, and no killing, yet. Clear?

DICK: Clear.

SILVER: But, when we do kill them, I claim Trelawney. And remember, dead men don't bite.

GEORGE: Ay, ay, Long John!

(ALL exit but JIM)

JIM: *(to audience)* Oh no! Long John Silver IS the one-legged man that Billy Bones warned me about! I have to tell the others!

(JIM runs offstage)

The Tempest for Kids

PROSPERO: Hast thou, spirit, performed to point the tempest that I bade thee?

ARIEL: What? Was that English?

PROSPERO: *(Frustrated)* Did you make the storm hit the ship?

ARIEL: Why didn't you say that in the first place? Oh yeah! I rocked that ship! They didn't know what hit them.

PROSPERO: Why, that's my spirit! But are they, Ariel, safe?

ARIEL: Not a hair perished.

PROSPERO: Woo-hoo! All right. We've got more work to do.

ARIEL: Wait a minute. You're still going to free me, right, Master?

PROSPERO: Oh, I see. Is it sooooo terrible working for me? Huh? Remember when I saved you from that witch? Do you? Remember when that blue-eyed hag locked you up and left you for dead? Who saved you? Me, that's who!

ARIEL: I thank thee, master.

PROSPERO: I will free you in two days, okay? Sheesh. Patience is a virtue, or haven't you heard. Right. Where was I? Oh yeah... I need you to disguise yourself like a sea nymph and then... *(PROSPERO whispers something in ARIEL'S ear)* Got it?

ARIEL: Got it. *(ARIEL exits)*

PROSPERO: *(to MIRANDA)* Awake, dear heart, awake!

(MIRANDA yawns loudly)

PROSPERO: Shake it off. Come on. We'll visit Caliban, my slave.

MIRANDA: The witch's son? You mean the MONSTER! He's creepy and stinky!!!

PROSPERO: Mysterious and sneaky,

MIRANDA: Altogether freaky,

MIRANDA & PROSPERO: He's Caliban the slave!!! *(snap, snap!)*

PROSPERO: *(Calls offstage)* What, ho! Slave! Caliban!

(enter CALIBAN)

CALIBAN: Oh, look it's the island stealers! This is my home! My mother, the witch, left it to me and now you treat me like dirt.

MIRANDA: Oh boo-hoo! I used to feel sorry for you, I even taught you our language, but you tried to hurt me so now we have to lock you in that cave.

CALIBAN: I wish I had never learned your language!

PROSPERO: Go get us wood! If you don't, I'll rack thee with old cramps, and fill all thy bones with aches!

CALIBAN: *(to AUDIENCE)* He's so mean to me! But I have to do what he says. ANNOYING! *(exit CALIBAN)*

(enter FERDINAND led by "invisible" ARIEL)

ARIEL: *(Singing)* Who let the dogs out?! Woof, woof, woof!! *(Spookily)* The watchdogs bark; bow-wow, bow-wow!

FERDINAND: *(Dancing across stage)* Where should this music be? Where is it taking me! What's going on?

King Lear for Kids

ACT 1 SCENE 1

KING LEAR's palace

(enter FOOL entertaining the audience with jokes, dancing, juggling, Hula Hooping... whatever the actor's skill may be; enter KENT)

KENT: Hey, Fool!

FOOL: What did you call me?!

KENT: I called you Fool.

FOOL: That's my name, don't wear it out! *(to audience)* Seriously, that's my name in the play!

(enter LEAR, CORNWALL, ALBANY, GONERIL, REGAN, and CORDELIA)

LEAR: The lords of France and Burgundy are outside. They both want to marry you, Cordelia.

ALL: Ooooooo!

LEAR: *(to audience)* Between you and me she IS my favorite child! *(to the girls)* Daughters, I need to talk to you about something. It's a really big deal.

GONERIL & REGAN: Did you buy us presents?

LEAR: This is even better than presents!

GONERIL & REGAN: Goody, goody!!!

CORDELIA: Father, your love is enough for me.

LEAR: Give me the map there, Kent. Girls, I'm tired. I've made a decision: Know that we - and by 'we' I mean 'me' - have divided in three our kingdom...

KENT: Whoa! Sir, dividing the kingdom may cause

chaos! People could die!

FOOL: Well, this IS a tragedy...

LEAR: You worry too much, Kent. I'm giving it to my daughters so their husbands can be rich and powerful... like me!

CORNWALL & ALBANY: Sweet!

GONERIL & REGAN: Wait... what?

CORDELIA: This is olden times. That means that everything we own belongs to our husbands.

GONERIL & REGAN: Olden times stink!

CORDELIA: Truth.

LEAR: So, my daughters, tell your daddy how much you love him. Goneril, our eldest-born, speak first.

GONERIL: Sir, I love you more than words can say! More than outer space, puppies and cotton candy! I love you more than any child has ever loved a father in the history of the entire world, dearest Pops!

CORDELIA: *(to audience)* Holy moly! Surely, he won't be fooled by that. *(to self)* Love, and be silent.

LEAR: Thanks, sweetie! I'm giving you this big chunk of the kingdom here. What says our second daughter, Our dearest Regan, wife to Cornwall? Speak.

REGAN: What she said, Daddy... times a thousand!

CORDELIA: *(to audience)* What?! I love my father more than either of them. But I can't express it in words. My love's more richer than my tongue.

LEAR: Wow, Regan! You get this big hunk of the kingdom. Cordelia, what can you tell me to get this giant piece of kingdom as your own? Speak.

CORDELIA: Nothing, my lord.

LEAR: Nothing?!?

CORDELIA: Nothing.

LEAR: Come on, now. Nothing will come of nothing.

CORDELIA: I love you as a daughter loves her father.

LEAR: Try a little, harder, sweetie!

CORDELIA: Why are my sisters married if they give you all their love?

LEAR: How did you get so mean?

CORDELIA: Father, I will not insult you by telling you my love is like... as big as a whale.

LEAR: *(getting mad)* Fine. I'll split your share between your sisters.

REGAN, GONERIL, & CORNWALL: Yessss!

KENT: Whoa! Let's all just calm down a minute!

LEAR: Peace, Kent! You don't want to mess with me right now. I told you she was my favorite...

GONERIL & REGAN: What!?

LEAR: ...and she can't even tell me she loves me more than a whale? Nope. Now I'm mad.

KENT: Royal Lear, really...

LEAR: Kent, I'm pretty emotional right now! You better not try to talk me out of this...

KENT: Sir, you're acting ... insane.

Macbeth for Kids
ACT 2 SCENE 1

(DUNCAN runs on stage and dies with a dagger stuck in him, MACBETH drags his body off and then returns with the bloody dagger. LADY MACBETH enters)

LADY MACBETH: Did you do it?

MACBETH: *(clueless)* Do what?

LADY MACBETH: KILL HIM!

MACBETH: Oh yeah, all done. I have done the deed.

LADY MACBETH: *(pointing at the dagger)* What is that?

MACBETH: What?

LADY MACBETH: Why do you still have the bloody dagger with you?

MACBETH: Ummmmm, I don't know.

LADY MACBETH: Well go put it back!

MACBETH: NO! I'll go no more! I'm scared of the dark, and there is a dead body in there. I am afraid to think what I have done.

LADY MACBETH: Man you are a wimp, give me the dagger. *(LADY MACBETH takes the dagger, exits, and returns)*

LADY MACBETH: All done.

(there is a loud knock at the door)

LADY MACBETH: It's 2am! This really is not a good time for more visitors. *(goes to the door)* Who is it? *(opens door)*

MACDUFF: It is Macduff. I am here to see the king.

MACBETH: He is sleeping in there.

(MACDUFF exits while MACBETH and LADY MACBETH look at each other)

MACDUFF: *(offstage scream)* AGHHHHHHHHHHH – He's dead, he's dead!!! *(MACDUFF enters)*

MACBETH: Who?

MACDUFF: Who do you think? *(they both scream)*

BANQUO: *(BANQUO, MALCOLM, and DONALBAIN enter)* What happened, can't someone get a good night sleep around here?

MACDUFF: The king has been murdered.

MALCOLM & DONALBAIN: Aghhhhhhhh!!!!!!!!

DONALBAIN: We must be next.

MALCOLM: Let's get out of here.

DONALBAIN: I'm heading to Ireland.

MALCOLM: I'm off to England. *(MALCOLM and DONALBAIN exit)*

MACDUFF: Well, since there is no one left to be King, why don't you do it Mac?

LADY MACBETH & MACBETH: Okay. *(LADY MACBETH, MACBETH and MACDUFF exit)*

BANQUO: *(to audience)* I fear, thou play'dst most foully for't. *(MACBETH returns)*

MACBETH: Bank, what are you thinking over there?

BANQUO: Oh, nothing. *(said with a big fake smile)* Gotta go! See ya! *(BANQUO exits)*

Taming of the Shrew for Kids

ACT 1 SCENE 1

(Enter LUCENTIO and TRANIO)

LUCENTIO: Well, Tranio, my trusty servant, here we are in Padua, Italy! I can't wait to start studying and learn all about philosophy and virtue!

TRANIO: There is such a thing as too much studying, master Lucentio. We need to remember to have fun too! PARTY!

LUCENTIO: Hey look! Here come some of the locals!

(LUCENTIO and TRANIO move to side of stage; Enter BAPTISTA, KATHERINA, BIANCA, HORTENSIO and GREMIO)

BAPTISTA: Look guys, you know the rules: Bianca can't marry anybody until her older sister, Katherina, is married. That's the plan and I'm sticking to it! If either of you both love Katherina, then please, take her.

KATHERINA: *(Sarcastically)* Wow, thanks Dad.

HORTENSIO: I wouldn't marry her if she were the last woman on earth.

KATHERINA: And I'd rather scratch your face off than marry you!

TRANIO: *(Aside to LUCENTIO)* That wench is stark mad!

BAPTISTA: Enough of this! Bianca, go inside.

BIANCA: Yes, dearest father. My books and

instruments shall be my company. *(She exits)*

KATHERINA: *(At BIANCA)* Goody two-shoes.

BAPTISTA: Bianca is so talented in music, instruments, and poetry! I really need to hire some tutors for her. *(KATHERINA rolls her eyes and sighs)* Good-day everyone! *(BAPTISTA exits)*

KATHERINA: *(Very angry)* AGHHHH!!!! I'm outta here

(Exits opposite direction from her father)

GREMIO: *(Shudders)* Ugh! How could anyone ever want to marry Katherina?!

HORTENSIO: I don't know, but let's find a husband for her.

GREMIO: A husband? A devil!

HORTENSIO: I say a husband.

GREMIO: I say a devil.

HORTENSIO: Alright, alright! There's got to be a guy out there crazy enough to marry her.

GREMIO: Let's get to it!

(Exit GREMIO and HORTENSIO)

LUCENTIO: Oh, Tranio! Sweet Bianca, has stolen my heart! I burn, I pine, I perish! Oh, how I love her!

TRANIO: Whoa, Master! You're getting a little over dramatic, there, Lucentio.

LUCENTIO: Sorry. But my heart is seriously on fire! How am I going to make her fall in love with me if she's not allowed to date anybody? Hmmm...

TRANIO: What if you pretended to be a tutor and went to teach her?

LUCENTIO: YOU ARE BRILLIANT, TRANIO! And because we're new here and no one knows what we look like yet, YOU will pretend to be ME at all the local parties. Quick, let's change clothes.

TRANIO: Here? Now?

LUCENTIO: Yes, Here and now! You can't stop this lovin' feeling! *(Starts singing a love song)*

TRANIO: Please, no singing. I'll do it. *(They exchange hats, socks or jackets)*

Oliver Twist
for Kids

(enter FAGIN, SIKES, DODGER and NANCY)

DODGER: So that Oliver kid got caught by the police.

FAGIN: He could tell them all our secrets and get us in trouble; we've got to find him. Like, in the next 30 seconds or so.

SIKES: Send Nancy. She's good at getting information quick.

NANCY: Nope. Don't wanna go, Sikes. I like the kid.

SIKES: She'll go, Fagin.

NANCY: No, she won't, Fagin.

SIKES: Yes, she will, Fagin.

NANCY: Fine! Grrrrr....

(NANCY sticks out her tongue at SIKES and storms offstage, then immediately returns)

NANCY: Okay, I checked with my sources and, some gentleman took him home to take care of him.

(NANCY, DODGER and SIKES stare at FAGIN waiting for direction)

FAGIN: Where?

NANCY: I don't know.

FAGIN: WHAT!?!? *(waiting)* Well don't just stand there, GO FIND HIM! *(to audience)* Can't find any good help these days!

(all run offstage, bumping into each other in their haste)

ACT 2 SCENE 2

(enter OLIVER)

OLIVER: *(to audience)* I'm out running an errand for Mr. Brownlow to prove that I'm a trustworthy boy. I can't keep hanging out with thieves, right?

(enter NANCY, who runs over to OLIVER and grabs him; SIKES, FAGIN, and DODGER enter shortly after and follow NANCY)

NANCY: Oh my dear brother! I've found him! Oh! Oliver! Oliver!

OLIVER: What!?!? I don't have a sister!

NANCY: You do now, kid. Let's go. *(she drags OLIVER to FAGIN)*

FAGIN: Dodger, take Oliver and lock him up.

DODGER: *(to OLIVER)* Sorry, dude. *(DODGER and OLIVER start to exit)*

OLIVER: Aw, man! Seriously? I just found a good home...

NANCY: Don't be too mean to him, Fagin.

OLIVER: *(as he's exiting)* Yeah, don't be too mean to me, Fagin!

SIKES: *(mimicking NANCY)* Don't be mean, Fagin. Wah, wah, wah. Look, I need Oliver to help me rob a house, okay? He is just the size I want to fit through the window. All sneaky ninja like.

Much Ado About Nothing for Kids

ACT 1 SCENE 1

(Enter LEONATO, HERO, and BEATRICE)

LEONATO: *(to audience)* I am The Governor. Governor of Messina, Italy.

HERO: Whatever, Dad. You are always talking about yourself. We know you're "The Governor". We've got it. *(sarcastically)* Governor Leonato.

LEONATO: Now listen to me, Hero. You need to behave yourself. We have guests coming. *(BEATRICE laughs at Hero)* And you Beatrice, you better watch your tongue, because I don't want you getting into a "war of words" with Benedick, again. Got me? Look, here comes a messenger.

(enter MESSENGER)

MESSENGER: Sir, I come to tell you that Don Pedro, the Prince of Arragon, his brother Don John, and his faithful men, Claudio and Benedick, will all be coming soon.

(exit MESSENGER)

HERO: Oh, goodie! I think Claudio is cute!

BEATRICE: Yeah, well, Benedick is NOT! He's always smelly after a battle! Oh look, here comes the smelly one now.

(enter DON JOHN, DON PEDRO, BENEDICK, and CLAUDIO)

LEONATO: Welcome, Don Pedro and friends! You have fought bravely. Please stay and party with us.

DON PEDRO: We will, thank you!

DON JOHN: *(aside and pouting to the audience)* My brother gets all the attention! I hate him!

DON PEDRO: Don John, what are you saying over there?

DON JOHN: Oh nothing, dear brother. *(starts dancing VERY badly)* Just practicing my dance moves for the party!

BEATRICE: *(mockingly to BENEDICK)* So Benedick, you're back again? *(sniffs him)* And, whew! *(plugging her nose with her fingers)* Smelly as usual.

BENEDICK: *(mockingly in a high girl's voice)* "Smelly as usual" You, my dear Beatrice, are a pain as usual. Are you ready to continue our merry war?

BEATRICE: You mean our war of words? You know it!

BENEDICK: You are such a parrot-teacher.

BEATRICE: What did you call me?

BENEDICK: Someone who talks A LOT! What's the matter? Forget your dictionary? You know, *(said slowly as if she doesn't understand English)* PARROT TEACHER.

BEATRICE: Humph! A bird of my tongue is better than a beast of yours!

BENEDICK: I wish my horse had the speed of your tongue!

BEATRICE: *(to audience)* Oh, he makes me sooooo mad! *(BEATRICE stomps her feet like a 4-year old and storms offstage)*

LEONATO: *(to audience)* There's a skirmish of wit between them. *(to all)* Everyone, let's go to my castle.

You know, the castle that belongs to The Governor? *(with two thumbs pointing at himself)*

(all exit except CLAUDIO and BENEDICK)

CLAUDIO: *(to BENEDICK)* Hero is sooooooo cute!

BENEDICK: Whoa, did you just say, "cute"? No, no, no, NO! A kitten is cute, a baby is cute, but her? No. With a name like "Hero", she can NOT be cute!

CLAUDIO: Yeah, what about her name?

BENEDICK: Come on. "Hero?" Does she drive the Batmobile and wear a cape, too?

CLAUDIO: Leave her alone because...because...because I think I want to marry her!

BENEDICK: Marry? Whoa, buddy! Listen, I mean, she's a bit..... plain. Actually, I do not like her. And as for marriage, it's overrated, so last year. You'll never catch me getting married. That's right, the single life for me!

CLAUDIO: *(CLAUDIO is day dreamy and lovesick)* She is the sweetest lady that I ever looked on. Could you buy such a jewel?

BENEDICK: *(to audience)* And a case to put her into.

(enter DON PEDRO)

DON PEDRO: Where have you guys been?

BENEDICK: You won't believe this! Lovesick Claudio here wants to marry Hero. Hah! Isn't that hilarious!?

DON PEDRO: Be careful Benedick, my friend. Remember, this is a comedy, and all of Shakespeare's comedies end in marriage.

CLAUDIO: Yeah!

ABOUT THE AUTHOR

BRENDAN P. KELSO, came to writing modified Shakespeare scripts when he was taking time off from work to be at home with his newly born son. "It just grew from there". Within months, he was being asked to offer classes in various locations and acting organizations along the Central Coast of California. Originally employed as an engineer, Brendan never thought about writing. However, his unique personality, humor, and love for engaging the kids with The Bard has led him to leave the engineering world and pursue writing as a new adventure in life! He has always believed, "the best way to learn is to have fun!" Brendan makes his home on the Central Coast of California and loves to spend time with his wife and son.

NOTES

Made in the USA
San Bernardino, CA
30 May 2018